THE
PATHWAY HOME

Poems
by
E. J. Ritchie
1874 – 1959

October 2006

Printed by
Antrim Printers,
Steeple Industrial Estate,
Antrim, BT41 1AB.

Published 2006 by S. Ritchie
11 Altinure Road, Claudy,
Co. Londonderry, BT47 4EX

ISBN 0-9554397-0-1
978-0-9554397-0-4

Contents

Preface

This collection of poems by the late Miss Elizabeth Jane Ritchie has been produced with the desire that it will be a help to Christians on their pathway home to Heaven. We know that our time here on earth should be spent wisely, as it is an invaluable opportunity for serving the Lord; it is to our benefit to heed any exhortation to greater service. We also know that our journey is not without difficulty, but we are thankful for the provision which the Lord has made for us: part of this is the fact that believers are to help each other. These poems, written by one who was a believer in the Lord Jesus Christ, should be seen in that context.

The poems cover a broad spectrum of subject areas in relation to the Christian pathway, from salvation itself to consecration, service, exhortation, comfort and thanksgiving. Our attitude to fellow-believers is dealt with, as is concern for the unsaved. Miss Ritchie draws spiritual lessons from men and women of the Bible as well as from the ordinary circumstances of life, and also from war.

It is sincerely desired that the believers who read these poems will be edified, exhorted and comforted on their pathway home to glory.

*   *   *   *   *   *

The help of the late Mr. Wynnfield Hooke of Lisburn in early work leading to this publication is acknowledged; he provided much appreciated assistance when the possibility of putting the poems into print was being explored.

Miss E. J. Ritchie

Miss Elizabeth Jane Ritchie

Miss Ritchie, who was known as Jeannie, came from the townland of Straid, near the village of Claudy, in County Londonderry. Born in 1874, she enjoyed a comprehensive education by the standards of that time – firstly at Tirglasson National School, then at the Misses Holmes Strand Ladies' School, Londonderry, Mrs. Byer's High School, Belfast, and Magee University College, Londonderry. For a period she studied in Germany, where she taught English in a German school. Later she held a teaching post in a ladies' school in Monaghan but after some time there was obliged to retire for health reasons.

Besides having a knowledge of German, she was also fluent in French, and this enabled her to render a special service when a little girl from the Dungiven district had to be sent to the Pasteur Institute in Paris for treatment for rabies caused by the bite of a mad dog; Miss Ritchie accompanied her there as interpreter. After the Second World War, when various charitable bodies were carrying out relief work in Germany and elsewhere, Miss Ritchie gave of her time in the translation of correspondence.

Miss Ritchie was a member of the local assembly of believers in the Lord Jesus Christ which was established in the Claudy district around 1902. She was revered as a lady of Christian character and saintly life, being one who lived in the presence of God; she has long been remembered by those who knew her. She went home to be with the Lord in 1959.

It had been known that Miss Ritchie had written poetry, with at least one poem being available, but it was not until 2003 that two note-books containing many poems written by her were found in an attic in Walsall, England, in the home of a relative. It is as a result of that find that this book has now been produced.

The MacCombe garden at Ballyarton, near Claudy

Pray for me

Pray, oh, pray for me that my life may be
   One sweet melody of praise,
That no jarring note through its strains may float
   In the dark and cloudy days.

That through storm and rain still the sweet refrain
   May to God's own ear ascend,
And grow more sublime with the course of time,
   More triumphant till the end.

Pray, oh, pray for me that my soul may be
   Like a garden watered well,
A rich fertile place filled with fruits of grace
   Which of care and culture tell,

Which is tended so that the weeds can't grow,
   Nor the cankerworm be found,
Nor the foxes small dare to scale the wall
   Which encloses it around;

Where the winds that blow make the spices flow
   And to pleasures pure invite,
And where every day my loved Master may
   Eat His fruit with great delight.

From Darkness to Light

I was a timid child and full of fear
For I was bound by punishment severe
Within a narrow groove. I dared not disobey
And I was so repressed in every way
That I seemed good, yet deep within my heart
Rebellion often rose with fiery dart,
And well I knew that evil lurked within,
That I was dead in trespasses and sin.
Away at school the laws did not relax
But in severity they seemed to wax;
Placid and calm appeared my outward life,
But all within was bitterness and strife.
I loved to go to church for there I found
Some respite from the ills that thronged around.
It was a pleasure, easeful, unrestrained,
To sit in comfort and be entertained.
The songs of Zion, soothing, full of cheer,
Filled me with visions of a brighter sphere
Where buffetings and hardships are unknown
And tears are wiped away, and not a groan
Is ever heard, where in eternal calms
The ransomed hosts wave their triumphal palms,
And sing the new new song, where cherubim
Do veil their faces as they worship Him
Who sits upon the throne; the city fair
With jasper walls and pearly portals where
The ransomed dwell, while o'er the shining ways
Bright angels pass. Enraptured I would gaze,
But then, the service over, it was hard
These lovely lofty visions to discard,
To tread again life's cheerless irksome way,
And suffer biting taunts from day to day.
But though my life was wrapped in grief and gloom,
And though the future held but direst doom,
I would not be a Christian; I abhorred
Those who professed to love and serve the Lord.

They seemed so strict, and narrow, and austere
That they repelled me. Joy would disappear
At their approach. My lot indeed was hard,
But how could I endure to be debarred
From every kind of pleasure and submit
To laws more stringent? Could I meekly sit
And learn from those I loathed? Nay, nay, I turned
Away from God, and His salvation spurned.
But then that pit of fearful agony
Loomed ominously ahead and frighted me.
I knew that Christ, the Father's only Son,
Was full of love, and died that He might win
Vile sinners back to God. I was distressed
Because His followers I did so detest.
Yes, God was great and good, then why, oh, why
Did He not robes of righteousness supply
To all His own, and dower them with grace
And every virtue till no eye could trace
A flaw? Were they what they should be,
Then they could win the sinful ones like me.
Yes, after all 'twas they who really barred
My way to God, and made His way seem hard.
    I did not want to dwell for endless years
Among the damned in agony and tears.
Then I began to wonder what I gained
So long as I on Satan's side remained.
What loss should I sustain were I to yield
My heart to God 'gainst whom it was so steeled?
He was desirous on me to bestow
His royal gifts and from eternal woe
Deliver me. He offered night and day
Divine companionship along the way,
And riches too, for I should then possess
A wealth of glorious golden promises,
And those fair visions which so often thrilled
My longing soul would surely be fulfilled,

A view heavenward

And in His presence I should dwell for aye
Amid the glories of eternal day.
Moreover He would not have me become
Sour, sad, and sullen, gloomy, grave, and glum,
But bright and joyous, hopeful, happy, glad,
In radiant Christian graces brightly clad.
This being so, why should I then refrain
From yielding unto Him? It was all gain,
No loss at all, and therefore I resolved
To be His child whate'er might be involved.
But how did this momentous change take place?
Would prayer and effort all my sins efface?
I then began to pray. I cried "Lord, save",
And wondered if He heard, if He forgave.
Long time I prayed. God did not seem to hear.
I lived in dread uncertainty, perplexing fear.
His invitation I had often heard;
It seemed too vague, but then the thought occurred
It was for me. To Him at length I came,
My helpless hopeless state my only claim
Upon His mercy. I accepted Christ
As my Redeemer; His precious blood sufficed
To ransom me. Then oh! what peace and rest!
I was no longer burdened or distressed
By fear of future woe. All, all was bright;
A glorious Heaven, a blessed Land of Light
Lay on before, and God was reconciled
To sinful me. I had become His child
A Friend was mine in whom I could confide,
A faithful Guardian ever by my side,
The clouds were lifted, all the darkness gone,
The light in all its splendour round me shone.
    Now I would fain have all my dear ones know
The good things God is willing to bestow;
If I could but induce them "taste and see
That God is good" how happy they should be!
They also would desire to spread abroad
The glorious secret of the love of God.

Ness Woods, near Killaloo

The Lonely Traveller

I walk alone amid the crowds that throng
Around me. Eagerly they haste along
Their divers ways, but oh! how very few
With me, a stranger, will have aught to do!
A number did some words on me expend
And showed themselves quite willing to befriend,
But soon our pathways shall diverge, and then
I shall have but the careless crowd again.
If love and friendship would around me cling,
If thoughtful friends would help in everything,
How pleasant life would be! Serene and blest,
In this fair world I then might seek my rest;
But oh! the way is rough and friends are few,
And pleasures swiftly flee when I pursue;
Privations, hardships, weariness and pain
My wishes aggravatingly restrain.
Yet He from whom perpetual joy-streams flow
Could make my path with light celestial glow
And set my life upon a higher plane
And teach me how to store up heavenly gain.
No longer in this lonely path I'll stray,
I'll turn to Him who calls so lovingly:
"O Saviour Christ, Thou holy sinless One,
I, a lost sinner, helpless and undone,
Now come to Thee, and Thee I do accept
As my Redeemer and my Lord. Safe kept
By Thine almighty power I've naught to fear;
Thou wilt protect and bless me while I'm here.
As for the future, all is glorious, bright,
For I shall dwell in Thy loved land of light.
What matter now earth's struggles and its strife!
I am redeemed; I have eternal life.
My Sun has risen, the Sun of Righteousness,
Whose beams shine but to gladden and to bless;
No longer shall I lone and friendless be,
I have a Saviour and a Friend in Thee."

The Acceptance

In her felicity so new and strange
She wept for very joy. Although no change
Was visible in her surroundings, yet
She scarcely for a moment could forget
That life had now assumed another phase
Because that morn the chain of girlhood days
Had quietly been riven. A few words said,
Acceptance, signatures, and she was wed.
How simple was the rite, and yet how fraught
With consequences vast! Long had each sought
That union blest while near yet separate
Their lives remained. His pleadings passionate,
His power, his riches, his munificence,
His noble rank, his yearnings most intense
Availed no whit; her prayers, her earnestness,
Her knowledge of his wish and power to bless,
Her confidence in him, could not effect
That union. Strange that nothing could connect
Those lives but acceptation vows! Strange too
How closely they were joined by words so few!
Each to the other had surrendered all,
No stipulations, no reserves, and no recall.
    Her husband had set out without delay
For his own spacious mansion far away
That he for her reception might prepare
And afterwards return to take her there.
Beneath the old paternal roof she dwelt
As formerly, yet constantly she felt
A strange new joy. Her outlook had been changed,
Her hopes and plans and prospects rearranged,
Her social status raised, her fears dispelled;
No longer were amenities withheld,
And all the time she had a happy sense
Of rest, security and affluence.

But though so many favours round her flowed,
Her heart was longing for the new abode
Where dwelt her lord, and 'twas her chief concern
To be in readiness for his return.

*   *   *   *   *   *   *

Her inward joy was so exceeding great
That glory-rays seemed to illuminate
Her dark surroundings, for that morning she
Had formed a glorious affinity
With One above. The restless period
Of separation from a loving God
Was at an end. She had been wont to pray
And beg forgiveness hoping to allay
His wrath what time she did not understand
His loving heart for, though the Fall had banned
The human race, she did not really think
That sin had altogether snapped the link
Between her soul and God. At length, when she
Perceived her cut-off state and destiny,
Her fond delusions having all been swept
Away, with contrite heart did she accept
Christ Jesus as her Saviour and her Lord,
And life-imparting union was restored.
The acceptation of that great love-gift,
God's only Son, immediately did lift
The fallen one, for from that act evolved
A union which could never be dissolved.
Allied to Him she would herself prepare
For that exalted place which she should share
With Him hereafter, and for her meantime
Earth was love-lighted, life a joy-bell chime.

A Song of Praise

O Lord of Hosts, the God of our salvation,
    We worship Thee;
Before Thy throne, in reverent adoration,
    We bow the knee.

Thy Name which is exalted, high and holy,
    We magnify;
We bless Thee for Thy Son, so meek and lowly,
    Who came to die.

O sinless Saviour, sin was laid upon Thee
    On Calvary,
When to that place Thy mighty love had drawn Thee
    To set us free.

Thy cross has made the very thorns that crowned Thee
    A laurel wreath,
The victor Thou, celestial hosts around Thee
    And foes beneath.

Redeemed by Thee and in Thy triumphs sharing
    So gloriously,
Thy robe of righteousness and beauty wearing,
    How blest are we!

Thy love, O Lord, Thy love our hearts hath ravished,
    To Thee we cling,
And of that love on us so freely lavished
    Would ever sing.

Touch Thou our lives, their music all awaking
    That each may be
One song of praise, one anthem ever making
    Sweet melody.

O may the music, evermore ascending
    In cadence sweet,
Rise till with seraph songs our notes are blending
    In bliss complete.

A Prayer

In Thine own presence, O my God,
　Teach me to linger with delight
Till in my heart is shed abroad
　Thy wondrous love, Thy glorious light.

Do Thou my life so permeate
　That others may Thy beauty see,
And that my presence may create
　In souls deep longings after Thee.

For souls are sad and weary oft,
　And need a presence to inspire,
A presence which has been aloft,
　To kindle holy pure desire.

Let me be such a presence, Lord,
　To love, to lift, to cheer, to bless,
To draw souls with magnetic cord
　Into the paths of holiness.

Grant me that soft angelic touch,
　That greatness and that strength of soul,
That gentleness and kindness which
　Can bring hearts under Thy control.

Grant that through me may be revealed
　The boundless riches of Thy grace,
While I myself am still concealed
　Within Thy secret holy place.

View from Portstewart towards Castlerock, with Donegal in the distance

A Prayer II

Lord grant me more glorious and great revelations
　　Of treasures untold that are stored up in Thee,
And fill me with holy and high aspirations
　　To claim all Thy love would bestow upon me.

May I live above all that is cold, hard and bitter,
　　Far far above hatred and envy and strife,
Too high to be dazzled by earth's golden glitter,
　　Too great to let meanness come into my life.

All by-ways avoiding, all crooked paths shunning,
　　No tampering touch giving inlet to sin,
Myself in the light of Thy countenance sunning –
　　That light which makes everything glorious within.

With meekness the highway of holiness treading
　　In shining white garments so pure and so clean,
Thy love and Thy joy and Thy smile ever shedding
　　A glory around me, a heavenly sheen.

Up, up in the realms of the lovely and glorious
　　Beholding Thy face may my soul ever dwell,
Where my love may abound, and my life be victorious
　　And in beauty of holiness seek to excel.

With princely demeanour and dignity gracing
　　My station in life, howe'er lowly it be,
Thine own loving hand all its plainness effacing,
　　Thy touch changing earth into heaven for me.

May I be adorned with Thine own radiant beauty,
　　With sweetness and gentleness, kindness and love,
And may pure holy motives transform every duty
　　Into some noble deed when recorded above.

I want, oh, I want that magnanimous spirit,
  That enlargement of heart that can freely bestow
With the bountiful hand which a child should inherit
  From a Father whose greatness no limit doth know.

I want, too, that firmness, that moral decision,
  That purpose of heart which will cleave unto Thee
In both small things and great with exactest precision,
  All selfish allurements refusing to see.

Yet I ask not that Fame should write down my life-story,
  I want to live quiet, obscure, and unknown,
And bring to Thee ever much honour and glory
  For making me truly a child of Thine own.

Thoughts for the New Year

How many times a New Year Resolution
   Has brightened up the future with the thought
That it would be the needed contribution
   To making life with moral beauties fraught.

Though hope soon fled, and though in acquisition
   Of grace-endowments I so often failed,
I need not lose the splendour of the vision
   Nor need my Godward yearnings be curtailed.

I can retain my lofty aspirations;
   They are like magnets drawing me up higher,
And they diffuse delightful emanations;
   And hopefulness, and zeal, and prayer inspire.

So I'll aspire to more and more compassion,
   To more and more expansiveness of heart,
I'll aim at living here in such a fashion
   As will repay me when I hence depart.

And I'll aspire to more of self-abasement,
   More power to comfort those who mourn and weep,
To more of kindness and of self-effacement,
   And deeper yearnings over poor lost sheep.

I want a shrine within all scintillating
   With gems of grace, where Christ my Lord may dwell,
A place whence beams celestial radiating
   Will of His own abiding presence tell.

The New Year full of promise now invites me
   To walk with her in garments pure and clean,
Her vesture so immaculate incites me
   To holy purpose, and to gracious mien.

I'll be courageous, and the New Year hailing
   With songs of gladness, and with smiling face,
I'll lean upon the Friend who is unfailing,
   And draw from Him the needed strength and grace.

My Talent

'Twas a bright little talent of gold
  Which my God to my care did entrust,
Which the Tempter, so sly and so bold,
  Wanted me to lay low in the dust.

And he told me it should be inlaid
  With bright gems made of genius so rare,
It would throw common gifts in the shade,
  And be held in esteem everywhere;

That it should be adorned and embossed
  With acumen, and learning, and skill,
Otherwise it would simply get lost
  Mid the heaps which the plain places fill.

And when weighed in the scholarly scales
  It should balance at least a B.A.
For a talent too light always fails
  An impression to make properly.

And he told me I meekly must hide
  Such a talent, so common and mean,
It was only presumption and pride
  Which induced me to let it be seen.

Thus with purpose persistent he pled
  With me never to use it at all,
Then I saw that he had fearful dread
  Of the power of my talent so small.

And he knew if he could but persuade
  Me to hide it, he need have no fear
For its beauty and brightness would fade
  And its power for good disappear.

Yes, he tried to make me through neglect
   Lose my plain little talent of gold,
And that talent is my intellect
   Which is cast in the commonest mould.

And this talent need not be abused,
   Need not foster presumption and pride;
It may just be as easily used
   In upholding humility's side.

For the owner can always apply
   It in any direction he will,
And upon his decisions rely
   All its workings for good or for ill.

And since God gave this talent to me
   To trade with, why should I give heed
To disparaging statements when He
   Knew exactly what suited my need?

And if only I trade with it well,
   If I use it as far as I know
For His glory, ah! who then can tell
   Whereunto my talent may grow.

Greater talents it also may touch,
   Greater powers in motion may set,
And may give them an impetus which
   Will more competent talents beget.

It has also the power to devise
   Means of scattering blessings untold,
And of winning the wealth of the wise,
   And that wealth is far better than gold.

Learmount Forest, near the village of Park

A Missionary Meeting

Near the little church in Learmount by the closing light of day
We met to hear a stranger tell of heathen far away –
A stranger who could only stop with us for one short hour
But who spoke with much persuasiveness and with the Spirit's power.

At first that reverend gentleman, the rector of the place,
In earnest supplication led us to the throne of grace;
He asked for blessing on us all and specially on those
Who labour hard in heathen lands amid the northern snows.

He next addressed us briefly, then he introduced his friend,
Mr. Stevenson from England who had come there for this end
To rouse a deeper interest in the mission work abroad
And make us more whole-hearted in the service of our God.

This gentleman then told us that the first thing Christ demands
Is not our gold or silver coins, our houses or our lands,
But a life that's wholly yielded to the service of the Lord,
And whose aim is Jesus' glory in each thought and act and word.

For if Jesus Christ is Master, if He is our Lord and King,
We cannot help but love Him more than any earthly thing,
Then all our worldly substance we shall view with different eyes,
As not our own, but only lent to us to supervise.

And we'll count it joy and privilege that we may have a share
In sending out the Gospel to the heathen who don't care
For the Christ who died to save them, and who never never had
A Bible with its light divine, and Gospel tidings glad.

A footnote to this poem says:
"The above is my first attempt in verse. Written Nov. 98."
This would have been before the commencement of the Assembly
in the district.

So these poor neglected heathen make them idols of their own,
Not knowing Him who loves them, they bow down to gods of stone
And they rend their flesh and suffer most excruciating pain
To propitiate the sun-god and his favour to retain.

He showed us poor Red Indian men who live so far from here
In the snowy arctic regions of the Western Hemisphere;
One of these was Sung, the chieftain, with red coat and long black hair
Who came to have his photo ta'en, and thought 'twas only fair

That he should receive a great reward for standing still so long,
But the artist took a snap-shot while he argued, so poor Sung
Had to go regretting sadly that he took the time to dress,
Yet all the while his photo was safe in the artist's case.

He showed us how, in that cold land, it does seldom cease to freeze,
And the ground's so hard that dead men must be "buried" in the trees,
How when tea is almost ready, they melt small white lumps which seem
Like pieces of wax-candle, but turn out to be the cream;

How the children in a bundle are securely packed and tied
At the horse's tail whenever they must go out for a ride;
How the mother sits in front of them upon the horse's back
And listens quite demurely to the screaming in the sack;

How the general mode of travelling at first sight seems very grand
The sleighs are drawn by many dogs at a swift pace o'er the land,
Of course you will remember that it's covered deep with snow
And it's on a beaten track through this the sleigh and dogs must go.

But it very often happens that one dog some game may spy,
Then off he goes forgetting the poor traveller in the sleigh;
He drags the others with him in his swift flight as he goes,
And soon all in rare confusion are o'erturned amid the snows.

Oh! what a queer strange medley then, as oft as this occurs,
Of dogs and man and traces mixed with sleigh and rugs and furs!
And yet the dog which caused it did not mean to be unkind,
He intended to go off alone and leave the rest behind.

He was in the line of duty where her chains bound him to stay,
But, like many nobler creatures, pleasure lured him fast away;
Thus we learn that sinful pleasures injure not ourselves alone;
Others too share in the harvest of the seeds that we have sown.

Then, when the scenes were over, he told us all to pray
To God to bless the heathen in those lands so far away,
And send His Gospel to them, and then with earnestness
He spoke of three short phrases which begin with C.M.S.

The first is "Christ my Saviour" for indeed we can't do much
To help the cause of missions till we know the Lord as such,
So it's very very needful that we each one should begin
With Christ as our own Saviour who has cleansed our soul from sin.

For if He is ours and joyfully we're trusting in His Word
We long to let the heathen know the peace He does afford,
So "Carry my Salvation" is the next command of His
And we joyfully obey it in the strength and power He gives.

Now whither shall we carry it? To lands so far away?
Yes, that's the last command He gave His servants to obey,
But if ties of His own binding still detain us in our home,
We should be just quite as anxious that our Master's kingdom come.

We should care as much for missions as if we ourselves were there;
We should be just quite as earnest and uphold them all by prayer
And then, too, in the homelands, we should faithful be and true
And ever do our Master's will, with His glory still in view.

If this is how we're living then we long to see the day
When our glorious Lord will come in power in heaven's bright array;
So "Come, Master, soon" 's the last one and we know ere long He'll come
To take His own redeemed ones to their everlasting Home

To sing for aye the praises of the Saviour they adore
And to dwell with saints and angels and with loved ones gone before.
Then let us be ever earnest, let us seek some souls to win,
Only to His faithful servants shall the Lord then say "Well done".

When the speaker had concluded, 'twas with pleasure that we heard
Our dear beloved rector rise to speak another word.
He said "If these poor people so much torture will endure
To please their cruel gods and make their future lives secure

How much more should we Christians do for our dear Master's sake
Who loves to give us peace and joy and the chains of sin to break?"
The rector spoke these solemn words, then he began to pray
And soon the meeting closed and we were on our homeward way.

And now just one suggestion ere I close this little rhyme,
Suppose that Christ as man to-day lived in that northern clime,
Suppose He wanted clothing would you not be glad to send
The nicest warmest garments you could make to such a Friend!

"Ah, yes", you say, "of course we should, great honour it would be"
But He says if we His brethren clothe, "Ye have done it unto Me";
Now when winter comes with icy hand and snowy cap so white,
Alas! too oft poor heathen find their clothing is too light.

And might not we in happy homes, by cheerful fires that glow,
Knit something nice and warm for those who shiver in the snow;
Oh, let us not for selfish gain that heavenly joy bedim
But realize the blessedness of giving unto Him.

Cast thy Bread upon the Waters

"Cast thy bread upon the waters,
   Thou shalt find it by and by",
Let Jehovah's sons and daughters
   This, His promise, verify.

Like the waters full of motion,
   Deep and dark beyond our ken,
Like the swelling surging ocean
   Are the restless hearts of men.

On these waters, tossing, heaving,
   Thou art called thy bread to cast,
With thy Lord the issues leaving
   Till the "many days" are past.

Thou art merely a dispenser
   Of His gracious gifts to thee,
Fill with prayer thy heavenly censer,
   Then bestow them lavishly,

Yet with great discrimination,
   And at seasons opportune,
Not with pride or ostentation
   Must thy precious bread be strewn.

Bread may break down prejudices,
   Petty jealousies remove;
It may stifle sins and vices,
   May create and foster love.

View from Downhill towards Donegal

It may heavenly scintillations
   Over darkened spirits shed,
And create deep aspirations
   For the true and living bread.

And thy Lord can sanctify it,
   And increase it manifold,
And to multitudes supply it
   As He did in days of old.

Should thy box of alabaster
   Be but homely barley bread,
'Twill bring glory to thy Master
   And a fragrance round thee shed.

The Workman

To passers-by the house did not reveal
Its age, for paint did skilfully conceal
The many scars of time, and though the roof
For many years had not been waterproof
The slates appeared undamaged, fresh, and clean,
And nowhere could a crack or flaw be seen.
Upon defects within I could descant
For I of these was fully cognisant
Through long acquaintanceship, and patiently
I had amended most of those that lay
Within my reach, but always too aloof
Without, within, was that defective roof.
It most annoyed me as I lay in bed
And listened to the dropping overhead.
And if those little drops had been content
With one small corner, my predicament
Would not have been so bad, but most expert
Were they in finding places to insert
Themselves the roof all over, making sure
Of my discomfort and discomfiture.
Just where the rain had made a right of way
And where I did expect it every day
Above the ceiling I kept dishes set
Which it could fill, but if when days were wet
I failed to empty these, then there arose
A multitude of baffling watery woes.
Poised on a box I changed the dishes, but
So narrow was the hole that had been cut
It was a skilful feat through such a gap
To lift and take them down without mishap.

On winter nights I dreaded every shower
And nervously would listen hour by hour,
And try to allocate the various drops,
And gauge their damage by their measured stops.
No use in rising till I really knew
They had decided where they would come through;
Then I would place a vessel underneath,
And hurry back to bed with chattering teeth.
Yet it was awkward sometimes when they chose
Beside me on the pillow to repose,
Or when they came, soot-laden, down the wall
And had resolved along the floor to crawl.
I had grown weary sending men aloft
Because the cheerful raindrops simply scoffed
At all repairs with putty, lead, and paint,
And quickly proved that these caused no restraint.
    High rose my expectations when at last
A tradesman, whom I fancied far surpassed
All others, came to stop the leaks. For him
I had provided bitumen and scrim,
But he rejected these for he was sure
That tar would fill each tiny aperture,
And quickly he the tar-brush ran along
Those places where he deemed that aught was wrong.
A few fine days of drought elapsed, and then
The drops, undaunted, all came back again,
But over these the tradesman did not fret;
On other kinds of work his heart was set.
A hundred little apertures to fill
Required but patience, neither strength nor skill,

The house which had the roof that leaked!

And none would care, and none would understand
Save one old dame, and so he quickly planned
Congenial work, work which my scanty purse
Did not approve, yet I was not averse
To his suggestions, especially as he
Assumed that trifling the expense would be,
And with delight my sanguine mind portrayed
The vast improvements that would soon be made.
It was the front which people would inspect
And paint could be applied with good effect.
The porch, some woodwork, and the garage door
Had all been painted just the year before
But these were done afresh. The gables then
Bewailed their general shabbiness, and when
These had been renovated, faded frames
Around the leaded lights made known their claims.
The door and door-case likewise soon revealed
Deficiencies which for a brush appealed.
I warned the workman well before he burned
The old paint off that I was much concerned
About the shade, and that he must repeat
The very same to make my scheme complete.
In everything I said he acquiesced,
And after having several times expressed
My wishes, I departed, feeling sure
That my delightful visions would mature.
Alas! On my return I could have cried.
The work was done; the paint had been applied
But in a shade from which my eyes recoiled,
And my so cherished colour-scheme was spoiled:
Where quiet colours did so softly blend
Henceforth would harsh and gaudy tones offend.

Then in one chimney was a jackdaw's nest.
My feelings toward it I had long suppressed
Because upon this man I had relied
To push it down when plastering outside.
When he had ladders up there I explained
How much that nest annoyed me, and complained
Of smoke that puffed down when a fire was lit
And through the windows made a slow exit;
My powerlessness to move it I deplored
But he my words complacently ignored.
And now he's gone and there the nest remains
And daily of the damp the room complains.
And many other trifling things annoyed,
And it seemed hard to have a man employed
To thwart me so, yet he did not intend
To be unkind; he wanted to commend
Himself, and though my words had small effect,
And though he listened to me with respect,
The work I wished accomplished he would shun,
And things I told him not to do were done.
    Now when that tradesman left, no doubt he thought
That he had splendid transformations wrought,
And great improvements skilfully devised,
And done far more than I had visualized,
But I thought otherwise. I stood aghast
Because the season for roof-work was past,
And many a wakeful night I could foresee,
And many a naughty drop tormenting me.
At first I felt indignant and irate
And thought it would be needful to vacate
The house; the passions which within me raged
All kinds of helpless misery presaged
Till at the Cross I knelt. The light from thence

Shone calmly down and stilled my turbulence
For in that workman I could clearly see
Myself reflected. Yes, he had served me
As I had served my Lord, and every shade
Of my own waywardness I saw portrayed,
And questionings arose. Had my heart yearned
O'er Christless ones, or was I more concerned
About the raindrops? And did I shirk
Some kinds of common tedious manual work?
And there was work which needed to be done
Upon my knees unseen by any one,
Had I been faithful in performing it,
Or made excuses when I wished to quit?
Had my one object been to please my Lord,
Or had I hankered after some reward
In human approbation? Furthermore
Had I imagined that I could ignore
Some small commands that I might do instead
Those things in which I was more interested?
Or that I could in some smooth subtle way
Gloss over selfishness and hear Him say
"Well done" at last. The search-light from the Cross
Revealed to me still more and more of dross
Until in utter self-abasement I appealed
For mercy and forgiveness, and did yield
Myself afresh for service to my Lord,
Desiring that henceforth in full accord
With His own will my work should all be done,
That His approval might be daily won
In every trifling detail, and instead
Of feeling hostile and discomfited
I am most grateful for the lessons taught
And for the deep contrition they have wrought.

Contrasting Fields

Here the prickly thorns and briars,
  Here the stinging nettles;
There the fruit the soul desires,
  There the fragrant petals.

Here the weeds are dominant,
  Here the sting malicious;
There the bush, the shrub, the plant,
  There the food nutritious.

Child of God, thy mental field
  Is with good things pregnant.
Shall it luscious clusters yield,
  Or shall thorns be regnant?

Shall the briars and weeds transgress,
  And the ground encumber,
Simply through thy carelessness
  Slothfulness, and slumber?

Keep, oh, keep thy field abloom.
  Tillage most intensive
It may need, but leave no room
  For the weeds offensive.

Pictures

We may with keen approval praise
　　The works of men artistic,
And think perhaps that Genius strays
　　In regions grandly mystic.

And that her sons, high on a peak
　　Above earth's strains and stresses,
Acquire perfection of technique
　　From her own light caresses.

And yet perhaps in some hard school
　　Those artists have been toiling,
While failures, flaws, and ridicule,
　　Their efforts have been foiling.

Against a stream of handicaps
　　They may have strongly striven,
Or chains of indolence, perhaps,
　　They patiently have riven.

No matter what has been the cost,
　　Or what may have impeded,
The struggling days have not been lost –
　　They have at last succeeded.

And art seems less and less abstruse,
　　And joy in work increases,
When they are able to produce
　　World-welcomed masterpieces.

River Faughan, near Park

As we upon their pictures gaze
    With thrills of silent rapture,
We almost wish that some bright rays
    Of genius we could capture.

And more intense grows our desire
    That we in larger measure
Might such artistic skill acquire
    And radiate such pleasure.

Yet something quite analogous,
    An art more worth attaining,
Lies in the power of each of us,
    Without artistic training.

And when aesthetic pleasures call,
    Ambitious yearnings waking,
We may respond, because we all
    Are auto-pictures making.

Depicting faithfully are we
    Our thoughts, and words, and doings,
Our picture evermore will be
    The sum of these accruings.

Our canvas is a sheet of time;
    We utilise as pigments
Our thoughts, ignoble, and sublime,
    And Fancy's flowery figments.

All, all are busy at this work,
   And all are energetic,
None even for a moment shirk,
   However apathetic.

And while with serious world affairs
   Men are themselves acquainting
And while they count up stocks and shares,
   They still continue painting.

It is not needful to have health,
   Or lack of things distressful,
Or learning, leisure, talents, wealth,
   Or ease, to be successful.

But all those who take pleasure in
   Delightful shades creating,
Can paint the scars of discipline
   In colours fascinating,

Can trace with graceful symmetry
   Lines caused by care and sadness,
And cover rags of poverty
   With dignity and gladness.

And when we sit where glory-light
   Is richly round us flowing,
With hues ethereally bright
   Our picture will be glowing.

As sunlight changes earth's drab dress,
    And makes it efflorescent,
So doth the Sun of Righteousness
    Make pictures iridescent.

To-day though worries round us flit,
    And though we sip vexation,
We may paint something exquisite,
    And worthy of duration.

We must, like artists, persevere
    Though we are teased and taunted,
We must not mind the snub or sneer,
    Nor be by blunders daunted.

We must let courage grow apace,
    And foster our ambition,
To win a high and honoured place
    In this great competition.

Adown the days still nebular
    We cannot e'en conjecture
What influence will float afar
    From our hand-painted picture.

When in the gallery of time,
    It is at last suspended,
May it be beautiful, sublime,
    And by our Lord commended.

Little Foxes

I had a book which I most highly prized;
'Twas out of print, and this fact emphasized
Its worth to me. I lent it to a friend
On whose integrity I did depend
But it was not returned. Hints were ignored,
And one direct request. Though I deplored
My literary loss, it was the slur
Upon my friend's exalted character
Which grieved me most, and which annoys me still,
And takes him down from his high pinnacle.
And he must first that valued book replace
Before he stands in his old honoured place.

*   *   *   *   *

He seemed so kind and ready to oblige
That we esteemed it quite a privilege
To have his friendship; he had been the same
To us for years; no cause have we to blame
Him personally, but we have been grieved
Because a darksome spot we have perceived.
We now will call him Paul. It is a name
Which none of our acquaintances can claim.
Paul had a friend he often went to see,
A man of wealth and generosity,
Who had an orchard, and who grew much fruit,
And Paul would bring his car and fill the boot
Betimes. One year when plums were scarce
The owner had so few he was averse
To parting with them, but alas! alas!
Paul came for apples; walking through the grass

He spied the plums, and to the great dismay
And chagrin of the owner, rapidly
His trees were stripped of plums by fingers deft,
And he was of his cherished fruit bereft.
It was a pity that Paul should besmear
His hands with plums for he was so sincere
In his desire to walk in wisdom's ways
And manifest delightful Christian traits,
Yet he seemed to be wholly unaware
That for the owner he should leave a share.

*   *   *   *   *

We are so weak ourselves, so prone to fall,
We dare not stand upon a pedestal
And harshly judge; rather do we feel
Compassionate because these facts reveal
Their heavy moral loss, a loss so great
That we its vastness cannot estimate.
And then the everlasting loss! Of it
We fear to speak because 'tis infinite.
And then we fear that we some trifle choose
And for its sake eternal blessings lose.
Such trifles are the foxes, wily, cute
Which spoil our grapes and all our luscious fruit.
God grant us henceforth wisdom, power, and grace,
These furtive little foxes to displace
From our domain, and may no other foe
Despoil the pleasant fruit we want to grow.

Forgiveness

When we with others come into collision,
  When rancorous and spiteful words offend,
When we are scorned and treated with derision
  By those whom we had striven to befriend,

Do we not hanker after some requital
  In sullenness, aloofness, or disdain?
Do we not feel our sufferings entitle
  Us to inflict some little darts of pain?

But such reprisals merely serve to nourish
  The roots of bitterness, and scorn, and pride,
And when these noxious weeds grow up and flourish,
  Their power for evil will be multiplied.

We must not listen to austere abettors,
  Who urge us to indulge malevolence,
For we are still ten thousand talent debtors,
  Though foes may owe to us an hundred pence.

If we forgive with certain reservations,
  If we some measure of our love withhold,
Then with exactly corresponding stipulations
  Will God's forgiveness unto us be doled.

If we forgive not, He may us deliver
  To rude tormentors, eager to degrade,
Beneath whose lashes we may often quiver
  Until the utmost farthing has been paid.

Although malevolence appears so ugly,
    Yet we ourselves in it would fain indulge;
We hope to harbour and conceal it snugly,
    As if its presence it would not divulge.

But in ourselves shall this sin be less heinous?
    Shall God or man this self-same sin condone,
Which seen in others does so deeply pain us?
    Has it in us a less malignant tone?

The fact that people are so irritating
    Is no excuse for us, but it provides
Grand opportunities for demonstrating
    That by His Spirit Christ in us abides.

Then how can we ill-will entirely banish?
    We ask God to remove it, yet it clings
Around our hearts; our foemen do not vanish,
    And we can hear their taunts, and feel their stings.

'Tis when before the throne, in secret kneeling,
    We bear them up, beseeching God to bless
Them bounteously, that love-waves softly stealing
    Into our hearts, will banish bitterness.

For in the light and warmth of Love consummate
    We see ourselves, and humbled to the dust,
We loathe our sin, and want to overcome it,
    And all our lives to laws of love adjust.

View over Straid and surrounding area

Be Great in the Sight of the Lord. Luke I. 15

Be great, O Christian, great in heart and soul,
And let the motives which thy life control
As far transcend those purposes which sway
Mere selfish minds as doth the light of day
All lesser lights. While Heaven's glory shines
Through all thy motives, purposes, designs,
Do not their wondrous magnitude display
Lest breath of pride should dim their radiancy.
These thrive in secret, therefore take good heed
To let thy inward greatness far exceed
Its outer seeming. True, thou mayest fall
And feel thyself so infinitely small
That thou canst scarcely dare to look upon
The face of man, thy self-esteem all gone,
But thou, in thy distress, canst turn again
To Him who knows thy grief, thy deep deep pain
And true repentance. He will take thy hand
And raise thee up, and make thee understand
How truly small thou art, and yet how great
As thou dost in His life participate,
That thou hast naught whatever of thine own
Since all thy greatness comes from Him alone.
And yet withal true greatness greatly lies
In thine own power. It grows by exercise
Of mind, and heart, and will; 'tis thine indeed
As thou dost choose, for nothing can impede
The course of thine aspirings, or prevent
Thy mind from having still its high intent.
If motives were alive and hovering near,
Should some of them in hideous form appear,
And others all resplendent with the light
That shines eternal, beautiful and bright,
Then, knowing that the latter would diffuse
A heavenly radiancy, wouldst thou not choose
Them for thy words and deeds, discarding all
Those which unworthy are, and mean, and small?

Yet such a choice is thine, and many a time
Thy choice may make the simplest act sublime.
But if thou fail in watchfulness and prayer
The loathsome ones will creep in unaware
Behind thy fairest deeds, and rob them of
The fulgency that cometh from above.
Thy secret motives all have wondrous weight,
And judgment scales are very accurate,
Be therefore watchful; daily, hourly, thou
Must some invite, and others disallow.
Thou hast no need to use a motive base
However well adapted to the case,
However strongly poverty demands
The use of it to carry out thy plans.
Thy God is wealthy, and, when needful, He
Will bring forth treasures from His stores for thee.
Think of His power with worlds at His command,
Think of His love, so shall thy heart expand,
Consider all the marvels of His grace,
And mount by prayer into His holy place.
From that high standpoint thou canst have a view
Of earthly things in their perspective true.
Seen from that eminence with vision clear
Will many things diminutive appear,
E'en earthly greatness, richly-robed, will seem
A transitory thing, a passing dream,
By inward greatness very far surpassed
For this will there assume proportions vast.
  Be great, then, Christian, great in heart and soul,
Let inward greatness ever be thy goal,
Let nothing drag thee from thy high estate
But let each noble action stimulate
Thy soul to greater things till thou outgrow
Thy hampered mundane state of embryo,
And suddenly emerging, winged for flight,
Soar up to dwell in everlasting light.

The Voyage

The south wind blew softly; their white sails they spread
Like great pinions, and lightly o'er calm seas they sped;
All was tranquil and fair, not a sign of a squall,
And absurd seemed the protests and warnings of Paul.

Though his words had betimes stirred up some little qualms,
They were lured by the glory of sunshine and calms,
And imagined that they could have nothing to fear
From a storm while the port of Phenice was near.

But abruptly the wind in a passion arose
And it woke up the sea from its state of repose.
While the waves rose like monsters in fury, it blew
Its loud sirens and laughed at the terrified crew.

Then they girded the ship though opposed by the blast,
And down into the waters the tackling they cast,
But the tempest still raged; they could feel its cold breath
As it thundered its threatenings of shipwreck and death.

Many days all the lights in the heavens had failed,
And they knew not their bearings, or whither they sailed,
And they dreaded the treacherous quicksands and rocks
While they constantly suffered from rude billow shocks.

Mid the fearful commotion their nerves were so strained
That no sleep could be had, and from food they refrained,
And they ardently longed for that quiet retreat
Incommodious but safe in the haven of Crete.

Then a voice calmly rose mid the tumult of waves
And dispelled their forebodings of watery graves;
It assured them that soon would their trials be o'er
And that not one would fail to arrive on the shore.

Portstewart Harbour

There is many a voyage and venture in life;
Winds are always uncertain and tempests are rife,
And though bright dancing wavelets alluringly call
One should wait – always wait for a signal from Paul.

When the south wind blows softly, hearts fondly surmise
That it augers success to their new enterprise,
And they loose all their moorings and gaily set sail
To encounter the darkness, the deeps, and the gale.

When the south wind blows softly, temptation is strong,
And the Christian is pleasantly wafted along
Into sin's darksome deeps, and the woe it entails
May be keen as that caused by euroclydon gales.

When the south wind blows softly, O Christian, beware,
For you know not the danger, you see not the snare,
But many a sorrow, disaster, and squall
Can still be avoided by listening to Paul.

Streamlet after rain

To a Farmer

All the crops had been good during weather propitious;
  Of a surplus to sell you felt almost assured.
You had sweated and toiled, you had been so ambitious
  Before winter arrived to have all well secured.

Though your servants each day had so much relaxation,
  You had none, and at night you felt weary and worn;
In your evening devotions you lacked concentration,
  For your mind was so full of the flax and the corn.

But these three weeks of rain have been most disconcerting;
  They have blighted all prospects of adequate gain,
And it seems to be hopeless to think of averting
  The privations which deficit brings in its train.

You had lifted the flax, but had no time for stacking,
  Yet your fears for its safety you constantly quelled
For the corn was so ripe, and the helpers so lacking,
  That to reap it you felt absolutely compelled.

And continual rain is now thoroughly soaking
  Both these crops, and you think of the way you had slaved
To protect them, and what makes it much more provoking
  Is the fact that the flax could so well have been saved.

There are maggots on sheep, and this helps to distress you;
  And the air is so stifling, the sun is so hot,
That its rare fitful gleams only serve to impress you
  With sure signs that your crops are beginning to rot.

And your peats are marooned far away in the moorland;
  Until transport is feasible there they must stay,
And you know thieves are rife in that barren obscure land,
  And you fear that your peats will all vanish away.

And you must pay the men; help is now most expensive,
    And on these rainy days men have little to do;
They create peevish pangs for you feel apprehensive
    Of more difficult days which are yet to ensue.

Fields that once were so smiling seem sour, sad and sodden;
    You can hear the loud voice of the streamlets in flood;
All the corn left unreaped is by rain-drops down-trodden,
    And wherever you go you are walking in mud.

But there's glory above. Your sad eyes may be holden,
    Like the eyes of the two who conversed with their Lord;
You may not recognise opportunities golden
    For the triumphs of grace which these dark days afford.

You must really admit you were somehow depending
    More on earth to supply you with food and with store,
Than on Him who has always His favours been sending
    Through the medium of earth, and a change you deplore.

It is not to-day's burden; it is that of to-morrow
    Which discouragement, doubt, and despondency brings.
O how foolish to conjure up phantoms of sorrow,
    And to quake at the thought of these fanciful things!

You are merely a servant; your Lord is imperial,
    You have only to do what He daily directs;
He provides for you bounteously all things material,
    And your confidence is the return He expects.

And though weather conditions put many restrictions
    On your harvesting work, and make losses so great,
You must count this as some of the small light afflictions
    For which glory eternal will well compensate.

You remember the children of Israel grumbled;
    For the lack of meat rations they wept and they wailed,
And the Lord was displeased, and they had to be humbled,
    And He sent fire and plague with the woes these entailed.

Let faith banish your great heavy load of dejection.
    Earth has shown you the fruits which depend on the rain;
Faith will show better fruits which may grow to perfection
    On these wet gloomy days in your heart's secret fane.

God is not a hard master. It is needful to test you,
    And to know if your heart round some idol is curled,
Or seeks praises from men, and He wants to divest you
    Of a craving for honour and wealth in the world.

Then be glad and rejoice. God is seeking to train you.
    Rise triumphantly over the worry and gloom;
See a Father's good hand in all things that now pain you,
    And His glory will all the dark landscape illume.

Mixed bloom in summer

Be of Good Comfort

Is thy sorrow too deep? Is thy heart aching, aching?
  And from tears canst thou not without effort refrain?
Yet take comfort for He who binds hearts that are breaking
  Has a balm for thy wound, and a cure for thy pain.

O remember His love which at death did not falter,
  Which shunned not the dark pathway before Him that lay,
And remember His love for thee never doth alter,
  And is planning the best love can give thee each day.

Tell me, was it not love which thy dear one enfolded
  That he felt not the chill of cold Jordan's dark waves?
And though Faith sometimes longeth for Sight to uphold it,
  Trust God's wisdom and love – 'tis for trust that He craves.

And rejoice that thy dear one is safe in His keeping,
  Far beyond all of suffering and sighing, and grief;
And when loneliness o'er thee comes mournfully creeping,
  Lift thine eyes up to Him, and He'll give thee relief.

Lift thine eyes up to Him and thy faith shall grow stronger,
  Lift thine eyes up to Him, and thy heart shall find rest,
And the burden that crushes shall crush thee no longer;
  Thou shalt only be glad that thy child is so blest.

When thou lookest below thou art lonely, so lonely,
  And the burden of sorrow is heavy indeed;
When thou lookest above there is naught but bliss only,
  And a Father to fill all thy heart's deepest need.

He will cheer thee with hope and with words kind and tender,
  And though weeping endure for a long painful night,
Yet the morning will come in its glory and splendour;
  Thou shalt meet thine own child in the glad morning light.

Is it not well worth while for the joy of that meeting
  To endure all the loneliness tearful and sore?
Is it not well worth while for the joy of that greeting
  To endure that on earth thou mayest see him no more?

Then be strong and take courage; though grief has been bitter,
  It has no sting of sin and no hopeless regrets;
To thy faith add hope's brightness, so shalt thou be fitter
  To acquire the sweet sympathy suffering begets.

Let no thoughts unsubmissive e'er rudely transgress on
  The deep calm of thy spirit to break its repose;
Comfort other sad hearts, and thine own grief will lessen
  And life's evening with soft benedictions will close.

Think how many beloved ones still cluster around thee,
  Think how many kind friends God has graciously given;
He has severed one link which might only have bound thee
  Far too closely to earth – now it binds thee to heaven.

Then rejoice in the Lord; wrap His comfort around thee,
  Let thy faith soaring upward triumphantly sing
Of His love who with goodness and mercy has crowned thee
  And from sorrow makes beauty of holiness spring.

Easter

Glad Easter morn! It speaks of resurrection;
 The earth revives and all her voices sing,
And bring to us afresh the recollection
 Of Christ's atonement and His triumphing.

We hear of Russia's arrogant intentions,
 Of bombs atomic, devastating, grim,
Of war which causes gravest apprehensions,
 But Christ is risen and we are safe in Him.

Behind the iron curtain men are goading
 Their dupes to deeds of fiendish truculence;
Their plots are deep and may beget foreboding,
 But Christ is risen, and He is our defence.

O let us be more lovingly united
 As dangers and disturbances increase;
By no harsh judgments let our lives be blighted,
 And no suspicious whispers spoil our peace.

The Lord is risen! As we imbibe the meaning
 Of these four words, and all that they entail,
We cannot harbour bitter feelings, screening
 Us from the light that shines within the veil.

The troubles and vexations that attend us,
 The causes of our jealousy and pride,
Grow very small beside this fact stupendous,
 And rude emotions rapidly subside.

The Lord is risen! Let us reiterate it;
 He lives, our Priest, for us to intercede,
And since through Him we are emancipated
 We sing with joy, "The Lord is risen indeed".

The Lord is risen! To heaven He has ascended.
 The Lord is risen! His victory we sing.
Soon will He come by heavenly hosts attended;
 The risen Lord will be eternal King.

Despise not .... little ones

"Despise not thou My precious little ones;
Although they grieve Me oft by heinous sins,
Yet are they children whom I hold more dear
Than wealth of earthly orb or starry sphere."

But, Lord, they are so very ignorant,
So full of self-conceit, and guile, and cant,
That they dishonour Thee; it is my zeal
Which makes me righteous indignation feel.

"Thine own self-righteousness dishonours Me;
Cast out the beam; thou art the Pharisee,
For on My little ones with scornful frown
From thy high pedestal thou lookest down."

But, Lord, they also look on me with scorn
And arrogance, yet I seek to adorn
Thy doctrine. I understand Thy word
Better than they; their tenets are absurd.

"Remember they have very much to learn;
Thine eye suspicious and thy manner stern
Goad them to bitterness; they only see
Not grace but self-esteem and pride in thee."

Lord, I have sinned; I bow me in the dust;
O give me grace my spirit to adjust
To Thy high standard, and to rise above
Reproach and scorn by lowliness and love.

Precious Children

Precious the sons and the daughters of Zion!
  How we would value them could we but see
All of them as they will shine by and by in
  Regions of light where no sin-spots shall be!

Frail earthen vessels we lightly esteem them,
  Made by the potter, made only of clay;
Vessels of gold, precious gold we shall deem them
  When they shine forth in celestial array.

Though they seem common; though we may despise them;
  Though faults and failings our eyes may detect,
He who has purchased them knows how to prize them;
  Grace can remove from them every defect.

Vessels of gold, yes, but gone is the splendour;
  Over them dust has collected for years;
Hopes of restoring their beauty are slender,
  And we are apt to pass by them with sneers.

Satan is pleased when we trample and squash them;
  Let us not further his evil designs;
O let us wet them with tear-drops and wash them,
  Wiping them well till the gold brightly shines.

O let us not at their blemishes grumble
  Lest we become as offensive as they,
Lest we should also cause others to stumble,
  And by critical contumely lead them astray.

Ours be the scrub-work, the cleaning, the dusting,
  Work which no plaudits, no thanks may receive,
Thankful that God to our hands is entrusting
  Tasks which the angels might like to achieve.

Precious the sons and the daughters of Zion,
  May our affections around them entwine!
O may they feel that they still can rely on
  Us not to soil, but to cause them to shine.

Old graveyard in Straid

The Burial of the Picture

O what grace divine in thy life did shine!
  O what bliss did thee enfold,
When the ways of God thy feet safely trod
  And His love thy heart did mould!

Then the peace serene of the word unseen
  Did thy life with gladness fill,
And the redolence of the air from thence
  Sweetly lingered round thee still.

And thy presence bright such a joyful light,
  Such a radiance did impart,
That thy picture fair I did always wear
  As a sunbeam in my heart.

Up above me far like a glorious star
  Thou didst sparkle, and I prayed
That thy life might shine brighter far than mine
  And its glory might not fade.

But with subtle wiles, and with winning smiles,
  Did the Tempter thee disarm,
And his hidden snare spread with flowers so fair
  Had the power thy soul to charm.

Not by paths of sin did he lure thee in,
  But by pleasure's pleasing call;
Thou art down at last, and the snare holds fast
  Though so gentle was thy fall.

Thou hast made thy choice to reject Christ's voice,
  And to stand in sinners' way,
And thou art so weak that a worldly clique
  Can thy thoughts and actions sway.

Has thy goal been gained? Hast thou bliss attained?
　Hast thou found one pleasure pure?
Nought but discontent with regrets all blent
　And a path of sorrow sure.

Yes, and thou hast found that the Tempter's ground
　Is a disappointing place
Where thou canst not rest but art still in quest
　Of the bubbles thou dost chase.

Others may not see any change in thee,
　May not mourn the glory fled,
But my heart doth ache as if it must break
　For my lovely picture's dead.

O the agonies of those awful days
　When I watched its flickering breath!
O the hopeless groan when I had to own
　That my picture lay in death!

I must bury it, I must now commit
　To the grave through blinding tears
In its lonely bier what I prized so dear
　For so many happy years.

No one else will know when I lay it low
　Though my soul be swept by storm,
For the obsequies on my bended knees
　All alone I must perform.

With a trembling hand in the silent land
   I now lay my picture fair,
But thou knowest not of that sacred spot
   And thou dost not even care.

O the deep distress and the loneliness
   And the aching void I feel,
While my sad farewell is the only knell
   At the grave where I sobbing kneel.

And yet as I weep in my sorrow deep
   O'er my picture loved and lost,
There is One to see and to share with me
   The tremendous burial cost.

And He comes so near that His voice I hear
   In a soft subdued refrain,
"Go not thou astray from the narrow way
   Lest thou too cause grief and pain.

Keep close close to Me, and I'll be to thee
   Of all joy and bliss the crown,
And beneath My wing shall no evil thing
   Have the power to drag thee down.

Do not cease to pray for that friend alway
   Who such anguish keen has cost,
And I may restore back to thee once more
   Thy loved picture which was lost."

Learmount Forest

Men as Trees Walking

See you men as trees walking? It is quite obvious
That your sight is defective if men appear thus;
Men can think, men can feel, men are not made of wood,
Men have souls, and for souls there is no finitude.

To the realms of the ransomed some journey along;
On their face is a smile; in their heart is a song;
You can give them encouragement, bid them God speed,
And for weak ones you can at the throne intercede.

But how many are bound for the darksome abyss,
Unconcerned about sin, hoping nought is amiss,
Walking placidly down the broad dangerous road,
And yet hoping to reach God's bright sinless abode!

Can you glibly converse with them, feeling no urge
To admonish of anguished remorse, should the dirge
Sound with sadness for them? Do you not even care
If they shriek day and night in a place of despair?

None can measure a soul. None can reckon its worth.
It commences its mighty career upon earth,
Then it passes beyond. Who can tell if your voice
May compel it to make of the next worlds its choice?

Do you look on these Satan-bound ones with contempt?
From obligation to them do you feel quite exempt?
Are they trees about which you are no way concerned,
When the axe lays them low, and the timber is burned?

It is true men may sleep for the Fiend holds them fast
And he keeps them well doped, but they might stand aghast
If the truth on them dawned. Might you not then essay
To contend with the foe and deliver the prey?

Men are passing your way. Let your eyes be alert;
See the jewels that lie 'neath the rags and the dirt;
See a soul with a world in the balances weighed;
See the price for a soul which the Holy One paid.

See you men as trees walking? O for keen piercing sight
To behold men as men in a pitiful plight,
Till your yearnings to save from disaster create
In your soul a great burden of prayer passionate!

Which will make you quite eager to spend and be spent
In endeavours to hinder their deep dark descent,
And the aim of your life will be just to save some
From the agony fearful of wrath yet to come.

Different Points of View

Said the jackdaw to his lady,
  "Darling, though we love to roam
Round the country, I am longing
  To possess a little home.

There's a very friendly auntie
  Living in a house at Straid;
Many small birds gather round her
  And they're not a bit afraid;

They reside within her garden,
  And she always feeds them well,
And I think it would be pleasant
  In that house with her to dwell.

We would not give any trouble,
  Would not even ask for food;
She should welcome nice companions
  For she lives in solitude.

She is kind to common sparrows,
  And I think she ought to be
Far more friendly and devoted
  To good birds like you and me.

I can see no valid reason
  Why she should at all demur,
If such civil honest creatures
  Should desire to live with her.

She might well spare us a bedroom,
  But one chimney for our nest
Will suffice us for the present;
  Auntie can keep all the rest.

Nests where they should be!

Does she really need a chimney?
 'Tis a dark and dirty place;
In a house so clean and tidy
 It is surely a disgrace.

And when smoke goes up that chimney,
 It is blown away and lost,
So to save it for dear Auntie
 Let us do our uttermost."

Said the little lady jackdaw,
 "Darling, you're a clever bird,
The idea is delightful;
 My emotions have been stirred

By your wonderful suggestion,
 And I think that pleasant site
Is ideal for our purpose;
 There no naughty boys could fright

Harmless unoffending jackdaws,
 And if we could have a nest
Full of lovely little babies,
 We should be supremely blest.

With the fascinating prospect
 Of a little home I'm thrilled;
Let us not wait any longer;
 Let us now begin to build."

So they rose up in the morning,
 And began without delay,
For to them this was a matter
 Of the utmost urgency.

But when Auntie saw two jackdaws
  Dropping sticks adown her flue,
She had visions of vexations
  Which would speedily ensue.

She protested very loudly,
  And endeavoured to impede
Their ingenious operations
  But to her they gave no heed.

Unremitting were their efforts
  The whole structure to complete;
Then they should be in possession
  Of a splendid country seat.

But alas! One day that chimney
  Speedily was cleaned and brushed,
And their lovely home was shattered
  And their joyful hopes were crushed.

'Twas to them a great disaster,
  And with intermittent groans,
They expressed their indignation
  In loud lamentable tones.

But they got no explanation
  And could never understand
Why their presence was not wanted,
  And their lovely nest was banned.

Now the jackdaws saw the matter
  From the avian point of view;
Auntie saw it from the human
  Side, and she required the flue.

Had they heeded her entreaties,
  Troubles might have been unknown,
And they might have had the sweetest
  Little darlings of their own.

Children sometimes, like the jackdaws,
  Have their cherished little schemes
Which are truly fascinating
  As they nurse them in their dreams,

And they look at consequences
  From their own restricted sphere
And they think that loving parents
  Are old-fashioned and austere,

And they heed not wise injunctions,
  And go on their wilful way,
Till they meet with disappointment,
  Or some great calamity,

Something which is all encircled
  With vexations and regrets,
Something which a train of troubles
  And anxieties begets.

Now of course a person's viewpoint
  Has a very great effect
On his conduct, and his conduct
  Has an influence direct

On his everlasting guerdon.
  Could he stand on heaven's height,
He should get a sense of values
  Which would guide his steps aright,

But in sacred Writ quite clearly
   Telescopic views are given,
Which reveal in true perspective
   Things on earth and things in heaven.

We can look adown the ages;
   We can see the fiery doom
Which awaits the Christ-rejectors
   When they pass beyond the tomb.

And the sight should waken pity,
   And should make us pray and weep,
And bestir ourselves to gather
   In the lost and wayward sheep

So that they might be no longer
   By the evil one beguiled,
But might turn and travel upward
   To the city undefiled.

We can also see that city
   Where the mighty King of kings
Reigns in majesty and glory,
   Mid exultant carollings.

And the prospect so alluring
   Of those scenes so bright and fair
Should be always an incentive
   To lay up our treasures there.

Looking from that lofty view-point
   We will grow alert and wise
To avoid the many pitfalls
   Which engender tragedies.

Which Side?

While bombs are being dropped and bullets hurled
And war-convulsions shake the warring world
'Tis strange that over all the troubled earth
Each nation's foes are merely foes by birth.
Whether they are aggressive and irate
Or unassertive and compassionate,
The German-born are all alike our foes.
Among the stern and fierce and bellicose
There may be many with delightful traits
Of character. But gentle winning ways
Appease not Britain's wrath. These help no whit
To gain her sympathy or to befit
The gentle ones for other terms than those
Accorded to the fiercest of her foes.
Because that nation is at war with ours
They must be numbered with the hostile powers.
It was not choice, 'twas birth which placed them there
And feelings do not count, nor character.
  And in the spirit-realms where only two
Opposing kingdoms are, 'tis likewise true
That all take sides according to their birth,
There is no neutral ground, nor is there dearth
Of subjects 'neath Sin's great heresiarch
For all are born within his kingdom dark.
He has experience, and manifold
Are his devices to retain his hold
Upon his own. It is his constant aim
To make them think that he will never claim
Their souls hereafter. Intermittent qualms
With pleasures or with pious rites he calms,
And if he can persuade his own that they
Are walking in the light, then he can sway
Them as he will. They dearly love to think
They walk in light while from the light they shrink,

They do love darkness; its soft shades invite
To revelries in which they take delight,
And darkness aids delusions; most of those
Who walk therein complacently repose
Upon false hopes, and bitterly resent
The least disturbance by enlightenment.
They feel so good they cannot understand
Why from the Father's Home they should be banned.
But not for rebels is that place prepared
Nor can its sacred joys with them be shared;
'Tis for the children, those who here on earth
Become the sons of God by spirit birth.
   O soul sincere, you hope and strive and pray
And struggle to believe more earnestly;
You are unselfish, kind, and generous,
But life, the great essential, comes not thus,
Nor can it spring from aught that you have done.
'Tis the reception of the Living One
Which life begets. It is for you to choose
Whether you will receive Him or refuse
His gift of life. But He must be received
As Lord as well as Saviour, else aggrieved
He turns away, and thus you can decree
Your weal or woe for all eternity.

Delilah and Samson

She dwelt down in a valley by Zorek's bright water
   In a warm sunny climate long ages ago,
As seductive was she as Herodias's daughter
   And equally skilled seeds of suffering to sow.

That she was but a fragile, a slim dainty creature,
   Her name, which means "delicate", surely implies;
She was probably also attractive in feature
   When she could gain Samson and make him her prize.

To get gain for herself was her first great endeavour;
   She was fond of their silver the Philistines knew;
She was also judicious, and loyal, and clever,
   And most persevering from their point of view.

Though for Samson himself she showed no kindly feeling,
   No concern for his welfare, no heart for his God,
Yet he still closed his eyes to her base double-dealing
   And excused her for plotting and practising fraud.

And although he did love her, had he done his duty,
   Had he kept himself true to his Nazarite vow,
Her character too might have grown into beauty
   And might not have been branded by all the world now.

To each other they might have brought gladness and blessing
   Had they only discreetly kept widely apart,
But alas! each wrought nothing but havoc distressing
   In the other one's character, conduct, and heart.

He was aged about forty, and much was expected
   From the judge and the ruler of Israel's land,
And great things he had done ere his name was connected
   With the one who so much of his time did demand.

And she must have been gracious and sweet sweet as honey,
   Must have made him believe that she cared for him too,
But she also encouraged the men with the money,
   And when Samson appeared, she could hide them from view.

When he came to her chamber she fastened around him
   The green withs and the ropes with her own little hands,
And there, helpless and weak, his strong enemies found him
   But his God gave him strength to escape from his bands.

Three times Samson escaped; three times God gave him warning
   And apprised him of dangers that lurked in that snare,
But, all protestations from God and man scorning,
   To return to the temptress again he would dare.

Yet his conscience struggled and fought with him bravely,
   And would not self-indulgence and pleasure allow,
Till he made up his mind he would speak to her gravely
   Of his faith in his God and his Nazarite vow.

Well he knew she was seeking his humiliation
   As she vexed and tormented his soul day by day,
But then why did he stand in the way of temptation
   When he could have so easily fled far away?

O what mattered to her great Jehovah's displeasure?
   Or what Samson should suffer of sorrow and shame
So long as the Philistines brought her their treasure,
   And among their great heroines gave her a name?

And what did she care that in God's sacred pages
   Should be written his story, temptation, and fall?
Or what did she care that adown all the ages
   The whole world should condemn him for telling her all?

So she feigned love and friendship, and seemed tender-hearted,
   And she soothed him and caused him to sleep on her knees;
There his locks were all shorn, and when strength had departed
   His strong enemies came and their victim did seize.

And they put out his eyes, and his feet they did fetter;
    They rejoiced and gave thanks unto Dagon, their god.
O how little thought Samson at first when he met her
    That Delilah could beat him with such a sharp rod.

So at last love of pleasure and lack of decision
    Had deprived him of friends that once loved him so well,
And had brought him so low as to grind in the prison
    And with many ungodly and wicked to dwell.

Did she pity him then? Nay, methinks she grew bolder,
    No clue to her feelings the story affords,
But was she not there as a smiling beholder
    When Samson made sport for the Philistine lords?

Was she not all along like a dark evil omen,
    The precursor of shame and discomfort and grief,
Till he fell at the last in the midst of his foemen
    And from sufferings disgraceful in death found relief.

But he brought down the house which so strongly was builded,
    And though sorely he suffered himself by its fall,
'Twas the dread dying shrieks of the people who filled it
    Which did all the beholders with terror appal.

O Would any dear Christian in his footsteps follow?
    Or Would any dear Christian make sport for the world?
Let him play with Delilah and find out how hollow
    Is her love when the darts of derision are hurled.

Samson fell and he suffered, and God wrote his story
    That His children of tampering with sin might beware,
That they might not in strength or in great exploits glory
    But be humble and watchful, and girded with prayer.

Walls of a city once under siege

The Chariots

All round the city was a warrior throng
With horses and with chariots. Bold and strong
And jubilant they were. No risks to run;
No fighting and no bloodshed, only one
Unarmed God-fearing man to apprehend
And woe to him who would that man befriend.
All exits were secured, and certainly
They hoped with ease to pounce upon their prey.
It would be simple, and so great a fuss
About one person seemed preposterous.
But while those men without the city paused,
Great agitation and dismay they caused
Among the citizens. What horrors loomed
Ahead on every hand! Could they be doomed
To all the sufferings of a siege which might
For weeks or months endure, and make their plight
Intolerable? But all forebodings fled
As quickly through the town the tidings spread
That this great army came not to molest;
It only came Elisha to arrest.
Elisha's servant plaintively bewailed
Their sad predicament. He quailed
At first. It was no wonder, for how could
One man oppose a mighty multitude?
The prophet, knowing God would intervene,
And, resting on His arm, was quite serene;
He prayed that to his servant might be given
A sight of fiery combatants from heaven,
Which when compared with Syrian hosts would be
Of infinite superiority.

That prayer was answered instantly, and lo!
The mount around Elisha was aglow
With horses and with chariots of fire,
Sure signs that God would manifest His power.
Elisha's first request to God had been
For opened eyes to pierce the earthly screen
Which hid the hosts of God. His second prayer
Was for closed eyes. It was Love's way to spare
Those enemies, so he asked God to smite
The Syrian warriors with the loss of sight.
Then all was dark and dreadful. Stupified,
And fearing with each other to collide,
They longed for some one who would take command.
Forth came Elisha. Boldly he could stand
Before them all and take complete control.
He bade them follow him, and not a soul
Demurred. E'en haughty Syrian officers,
Glad not to be detained in sepulchres,
Meekly obeyed. O what a retinue
Elisha had that day! And what a new
Strange spectacle. A multitude
Of sightless Syrian soldiers surely would
Stir up a great hubbub. Elisha led them all
Into Samaria, then did he call
On God to give them sight, and all at once
Their eyes were opened. How they would evince
Their thankfulness! Though Israel's king
Was moved to smite these captives, no such thing
Elisha would allow, but he requested food
For all these weary ones. With gratitude
They eagerly did eat and drink, then they
To their own longed-for land were sent away.

O child of God, when troubles round you throng,
When you feel low, and everything goes wrong,
Look up and see the fiery chariots,
The special ones that God to you allots,
Which suit your need exactly, and will lift
You far aloft till God's own gift
Of peace shall calm your soul. Your case may be
Unprecedented and bewildering, but He
Has infinite resources and will send
His horses and His chariots to defend
His faithful servant and defeat the foe,
And He can turn your strange imbroglio
To glorious victory. Then do not fear,
Look up until His chariots appear,
And don't forget that God can foil the plans
Of modern foes as well as Syrians
Of ancient times.

Queen Vashti

In the days of pomp and splendour
  In the olden olden time,
There was once a royal banquet
  Held in Shushan's sunny clime.
All who dwelt in Shushan's palace
  Were invited, small and great,
By the famed Ahasuerus
  To that festival of state.

Through the perfumed palace gardens
  To the large and spacious court
Which then blazed with regal splendour
  Did the people all resort.
There stood stately marble pillars
  With their rings of silver bright,
And by these hung costly hangings,
  Green and violet and white.

There the pavement was of marble,
  Black and white, and blue, and red,
And of gold in divers fashions
  Were the drinking vessels made;
Royal wine was in abundance
  On the tables where they dined,
And on gold and silver couches
  Princely potentates reclined.

Seven joyful days they feasted,
  Then his majesty desired
That the queen should come before them
  In her robes of state attired;
On her head, in glittering splendour,
  Shushan's royal golden crown,
Precious gems and jewels sparkling
  On her gorgeous purple gown.

'Twere the happy culmination,
  'Twere the crowning joy of all,
When her queenly grace should win them,
  And her loveliness enthral,
When, amid a hush of wonder,
  Vashti, fairest of the fair,
In magnificence unrivalled
  Should appear before them there.

What amaze and disappointment
  When the queen refused to come!
Was it just a fit of anger?
  Was it just a passing whim?
She had dared to scorn the summons
  Of her great imperial lord,
Such disdainful disobedience
  He resented and abhorred.

Strong his anger waxed within him;
  He felt humbled and abased,
For by Vashti's disobedience
  He was publicly disgraced.
Then his stern decree resounded;
  Henceforth he would her ignore,
His august and royal presence
  She should never enter more.

She should leave that place of honour,
  Quit the palace in disgrace;
Soon another and a better
  Would be asked to fill her place.
Deep regrets and heart-felt sorrow,
  Scalding tears of penitence,
These availed not; she must suffer
  For her deep and dire offence.

Now the Christian may be tested
  Like that hapless queen of old,
And his place of power and usefulness
  For paltry trifles sold.
He may hear his Master calling,
  He may dare to disobey,
His unhappy choice resulting
  In a great catastrophe.

Soft that voice may be and gentle
　　In the midst of life's routine,
"Come, my child, and let the beauty
　　Of thy Lord on thee be seen;
All those lovely Christian graces
　　Which so scintillate and shine,
I would have thee now exhibit
　　As a princely child of Mine.

Though I call thee at this moment
　　To a dwelling mean and poor,
Put on all thy best and brightest
　　For that little place obscure;
This is where today I test thee;
　　If thou do Me honour here,
Then one day I may command thee
　　'Mid the great ones to appear.

Wilt thou slight Me?
　　Wilt thou fail Me?
　　Shall My Name dishonoured be?
Then to fill that place of honour
　　I shall have no need of thee;
From thine eminent position
　　I must surely cast thee down,
Some one else will do My bidding,
　　Some one else will wear thy crown."

O we cannot gauge the issues
   Of refusing such a call,
Cannot estimate the depth to which
   A saint may quickly fall,
Nor can we conceive the honours,
   In a far more glorious sphere,
Which await all those who fail not
   In the times of testing here.

Ephraim

Ephraim is joined to his idols,
    Let him, oh, let him alone,
He is led, as are steeds by their bridles,
    Into pathways unsafe and unknown.

His heart is enthralled by their beauty,
    His will by their presence made weak,
He grows more and more careless of duty
    That he his loved idols may seek.

He knows it is wrong yet he lingers
    To taste of the pleasures of sin,
To feel the soft touch of its fingers
    And let it its havoc begin.

God's word has been telling him often
    "The way of transgressors is hard";
Does he think that his idols will soften
    That way, or from sorrow him guard?

Ah no, yet he waits not to reason;
    His heart on his idols is set,
Indulging desires for a season
    All heedless of warning or threat.

He knows that sin's whirlpool has suction,
    But pleasure has made him inert,
He will not give ear to instruction
    And cannot disaster avert.

River Faughan at Drumahoe

For his pathway leads down to the river,
  To the place where the eddy is strong,
And the coldness and damp make him shiver
  Though he joins in the laughter and song.

Many friends who strove hard to detach him
  From his idols, now look on aghast,
But no hand from his fate now can snatch him,
  He is down in the whirlpool at last.

Ephraim is mocked by each idol,
  Let him, oh, let him alone,
Since he yielded to things suicidal
  Let him suffer and sorrow and groan.

Insect with tiny agile wings

The Lord's "Great Army"

The Lord's great army! Went His fiat forth
To summon all the mighty ones of earth
Against offending Israel? Did He proclaim
The advance of legions in Jehovah's name
By sirens from the skies? Did He command
His hurricanes to sweep through all the land
And hurl fierce havoc with sepulchral roar
O'er fairest scenes, or bid the clouds downpour
Irate torrential floods that He thereby
The march of warring hosts might signify?
Sent He swift lightnings with destructive flash
Or mighty thunderbolts with fearful crash
From scowling skies? Or did His hand
With terrorizing earthquakes shake the land?
Did quivering mountains belch forth smoke and fire
And streams of burning lava to inspire
Alarm at His approach, and to impress
Upon frail puny men the awfulness
Of His explosives, heralds of the sword
Of mighty armies marshalled by the Lord?
No, not by booming of artillery
Or by spectacular display chose He
To blazon His advance, nor did He draw
Recruits from monsters that would overawe
And dwarf the quaking renegades. Nay, nay,
He chose the gentle but effective way.

 On cankerworms and palmerworms so small
And fragile little locusts did He call.
These round His glorious banner promptly swarmed;
Of these He his intrepid legions formed.

No bugle-call was heard, no beat of drum,
No clang of armour – nothing but the hum
Of tiny agile wings as steadily
This mighty army, to the great dismay
Of Israel, went marching on. The hand
Of man was ineffective to withstand
The advancing hosts. Before them lay
The smiling land, luxurious in array,
Behind them, barrenness, and soon a pall
Instead of living green, enshrouded all.
But though His army had caused such distress,
Jehovah loved that land, and yearned to bless,
And Hope resumed her strains triumphant when
He promised to restore those years again.

   That happened long ago in Palestine,
Yet frequently we see how Love divine
Makes use of unobtrusive armies still
His purposes of conquest to fulfil.

   His gracious sympathetic Hand refrains
From crushing blows, from sudden fearful strains
If gentler means suffice. If warning word
Has no effect on children who have erred
Oh, then, it may be He must have recourse
To His great army that He may enforce
Subjection to His laws. Dark moving swarms
Of tiny odious crawling cankerworms
Will by persistent gnawing soon consume
The pleasant things which made life all abloom;
Abundance and felicity they find,
Aridity and gloom they leave behind.
Their baneful work can cast a deadly pall
Of darkness and depression over all.

Yet God is love. His purpose is to bless.
His chosen ones must not His laws transgress,
He therefore casts o'er mundane things decay,
And blights fair blooms of happiness that they
May upward turn for their supplies, and learn
That soul-nutrition is their chief concern.
Rich soul-provisions which will never cloy
He wants them in abundance to enjoy,
And while they sit at banquetings unseen
Earth will resume her festive robe of green.

Ness Woods

Angel Guests

It must have been a thrilling moment when
Elijah woke to find a denizen
Of glory-land beside him, and to hear
The words "Arise and eat". How it would cheer
The weary prophet in his loneliness,
And all his hopeless grievances redress!
How he would value God's solicitude
In sending him the water and the food,
And a companion of the cherubim
To comfort and to minister to him!
And after that delightful interview
How joyfully would he his course pursue!
   Elijah was a mighty man who stood
For God before the world, a man endued
With powers supernal which would well equip
His mind for sweet and holy fellowship
With Heaven's ambassador. 'Twas meet that he
Should have an angel-guest for company.
   I'm vastly different, unworthy, base,
And insignificant, and common-place,
But when He sees it needful, could it be
That God would send an angel bright to me?
I dogmatise not, but I love to fling
My fancy round those visitors who bring
Me God's good gifts, and in these dear ones see
God's angels sent to minister to me.
They have a sweet celestial aura, though
They travel through the world incognito.
They come in plain terrestrial attire;
They have no wings, they bear no golden lyre,
But in their hearts there is a holy shrine,
A radiant place, meet for a Guest divine;
I glimpse seraphic splendours which one day
Will burst through all the covering of clay.

I see them as they are in Christ, all fair
And lovely, and this makes me more aware
Of my unworthiness; it stimulates
My love for them, and in my heart creates
A sense of reverence. With feet unshod
I close my closet, and give thanks to God
For each one, and for opening mine eyes
To see the glory through the earthly guise.
   These guests ethereal frequently supply
Those longed-for things which money cannot buy.
They bring such luxuries as cake and cream
And chocolate biscuits, dainties which I deem
Beyond my reach. Continuance of these
Delightful gifts I do not wish, though they may please
My palate, rather would I have them sent
Less amply-covered boards to supplement.
   Most highly I appreciate each gift;
The thankfulness, and pleasure, and uplift
It brings, words can't express; nor can scales weigh
These precious precious presents properly,
Because much time and trouble, thought and care,
So many details, and so much of prayer
Are wrapped around them. Thanks, best thanks to all
The angel-visitors who on me call.
   I would impress on all those dear ones who
Have been so kind and lavish hitherto,
That they are quite as welcome, quite as fair
When they come empty-handed. I'm aware
Of generous desires, but my heart craves
For friendship only; other gifts it waives.
God bless them all. May His good hand restore
Their gifts an hundred fold, and more and more
Increase their joy. May they grow more alert
To hear His still small voice, and more expert
In serving Him, and an exceeding weight
Of lasting wealth may they accumulate.

Visitors

The joys of friendship had been doled
  To me in weekly handfuls merely,
And I had hoarded them as gold
  And treasured each one very dearly.

It therefore caused an inward glee,
  A feeling of exhilaration,
When two dear friends came in to tea,
  And stayed for hours of conversation.

We shared our pleasures and our woes,
  About our work we made suggestions;
Our pains we tried to diagnose;
  We asked and answered many questions.

'Twas all so commonplace, and yet
  It made our friendship deeper, stronger,
And I was glad, so glad we met,
  And sorry they could not stay longer.

And oh! they left behind a rare
  Delightful fragrance of their Master,
And Friendship seemed to grow more fair,
  And her sweet influence grew vaster.

It had been pleasant to survey
  Those lives made rich by self-denials;
It stimulated me to pray
  And sympathise in all their trials.

For Friendship had with gentle hand
  Alleviated cares and troubles,
And we had learned to understand
  The way in which she pleasures doubles.

Thank God, thank God for those dear friends,
  The choice ones He to me has given,
Thank God that when life's journey ends
  Our friendship will mature in heaven.

Peats

A Present of Peats

I've told already how God sometimes sendeth
    An angel with a special gift for me,
And how my heart His goodness comprehendeth
    Through such benign angelic ministry.

When God sends angels on a mundane errand,
    They never think that precious time is lost,
And neither ease nor storm is a deterrent,
    Nor of the petrol do they count the cost.

This day was wintry; darksome clouds were scowling
    Upon a landscape deeply draped in snow;
An icy wind through leafless trees was howling,
    And in the house the temperature was low,

Because an oil-stove only I was burning;
    Peats were too scarce for ordinary use,
And for some time I had been sadly learning
    That it was needful peat-fires to reduce.

Then at the door appeared a smiling angel,
    And he was bringing fuel made of peat;
His presence with his load at once did change all
    My gloomy prospects with regard to heat.

Despite the earthly garments he was wearing,
    I saw the glory shining from within,
And though a peaty burden he was bearing,
    I felt God near as he was coming in.

Now peats are useless till they are ignited,
    So he brought also oil and kindling wood,
And no desire had he to be requited,
    Nor was he even wanting gratitude.

O, well I know the great expense and trouble
  Of getting peats, and I would gladly pay,
But that would hurt. I'd like to pay him double,
  But God will do it in a better way.

Then when he had deposited his burden,
  Since he would not his visit here prolong,
Immediately his tuneful voice I heard in
  The most inspiring thrilling sacred song.

But even angels, while their Master serving,
  Must not delay; they must redeem the time,
And therefore he, celestial laws observing,
  At once departed leaving thoughts sublime.

Had someone wanted me to give an order
  For something most desirable just then,
I would have liked to get a tape-recorder
  That I might hear that music o'er again.

Now though the peats gave me much satisfaction,
  And though I happened to be just in need,
I valued more the kind unselfish action,
  And thoughtfulness which prompted such a deed.

My gratitude knows no restraining measure;
  The cash-price of the peats it far exceeds;
For many many days they'll give me pleasure,
  And be a stimulant to kindly deeds.

Upon the spikenard Christ was not dependent;
  He prized far more the woman's love and tears;
Her motive made her deed become resplendent,
  And kept it shining all adown the years.

And so this peaty act I have recorded
    That others may be urged to deeds benign,
And by the Lord's "Well done" may be rewarded
    For doing something which will brightly shine.

But this requires divine discrimination
    For pampered ones on kindness like to feed,
And any motives of self-exaltation
    Will cause a canker in the fairest deed.

'Tis sweet to think that God has angel legions
    Who in His service fly at His command
Far o'er the world through vast uncharted regions
    But oh! the joy to find some close at hand!

'Coterie' of birds

Birds

In proximity close there's a large coterie
Of artistes who provide entertainment for me –
Artistes of a friendly and sociable kind
Who are not to professional duties confined.

Elevated their themes, and inspiring their lays;
With exuberant gladness they sing to the praise
Of their glorious Creator, and thoughts they instil
Of His exquisite handiwork, marvellous skill.

In this gentle society one can be sure
Of imbibing the things that are lovely and pure,
And where all are so modest, genteel, and refined,
One must learn to be constantly courteous and kind.

O thanks, thanks be to God for a home small and neat,
For the winged entourage which makes all so complete,
For the sunshine and shadows and paeans of praise,
And the beautiful thoughts which through these He conveys.

The Snowstorm

Silently, solemnly earthward they floated,
  Ceaselessly falling by day and by night,
Patiently earth with a deep layer they coated,
  Making it beautiful, downy, and white.

Blithe little breezes then whispered together –
  Whispered of sports in a grandiose style;
Hurricane sports in this dry frosty weather
  Would so enliven the world for a while.

Quickly they ran and their forces they mustered,
  Caught up the flakes, flung them high in the air,
Whirled them afar while they bellowed and blustered,
  Ready the wildest of antics to dare.

O it was fun with the snow-flakes to frolic,
  To tease them, and toss them, and with them to race,
To roar round the houses, and through the trees rollick,
  And all living creatures to frighten and chase.

Wildly they revelled and rattled and rumbled,
  They ransacked the corners, down chimneys they peered,
Any corn-stacks unstable they ruthlessly tumbled
  As over the country they madly careered.

Shrieking and shouting for days they ran riot,
  Causing disaster, and worry, and woe,
And leaving behind them, when all became quiet,
  Everywhere miniature mountains of snow.

When the hubbub had ceased, to our great consternation
   Not a voice could be heard, not a soul could be seen,
Snowy drifts had created a strange isolation,
   Having not left a path where the broad road had been.

Light little flakes had collected in legions
   Changing the scene and obstructing the roads,
Making our land like the white polar regions,
   Caging us close in our snow-girt abodes.

Myriad snow-heaps held up all the traffic
   Keeping the business-world all out of gear,
Hindering repairs to the wires telegraphic,
   Stopping all mails that were due to come here.

Men started shovelling snow on the highways,
   Gangs of them worked till a pathway was cleared;
Snowdrifts complacently lay in the bye-ways
   Till the thaw came – then they all disappeared.

Gone were the flakes but in dark clayey closets,
   Safe from marauders, preserved from decay,
They had left precious plant-feeding deposits
   Which would for damages amply repay.

Not with emotions irate or lugubrious,
   Had we these scenes so majestic beheld,
No, we thanked God for His winds so salubrious,
   Praised Him because they had microbes expelled.

He Himself sent them to make this invasion,
  His was the word which had summoned recruits,
By His decree on this special occasion
  They had descended in white parachutes.

Fragile and small each appeared yet He chose them,
  Bade them go in and possess all the land,
Man, puny man, had no strength to oppose them,
  Helplessly man their aggressive feats scanned.

If on our side as belligerent forces
  His mighty armies the Lord would command,
Enemies, lacking resistive resources,
  Could not the terrible onslaught withstand.

If we would turn unto Him as a nation,
  If we proved worthy His favour to claim,
Then would this war be of shorter duration,
  And all the glory would be to His Name.

Spring

All the rural bells ring at thy coming, O Spring;
   All the alar artistes rise to meet thee,
And with rapturous strains and with thrilling refrains,
   And with paeans exuberant greet thee.

But not only in song from the avian throng
   Comes a greeting. From thousands of voices
Other glad kinds of sound emanate all around
   To proclaim that creation rejoices.

Rosy splendour of skies at the early sunrise,
   Rich luxuriant fresh vegetation,
The serene atmosphere, and the music so clear,
   Cause a sense of delightful elation.

Many butterflies gay over blossom and spray,
   In the sunlight are leisurely flitting,
And industrious bees hum in gardens and trees,
   While gay posies are perfume emitting.

In robes handsome and new of an emerald hue
   Thou dost clothe all the things arboraceous,
And with patience and skill birdies secretly fill
   With bird-babies tree-pockets capacious.

Welcome bright harbinger of a spring-time more fair
   When shall come a New Order pacific,
When the sceptre benign of a Ruler divine
   Shall make earth an abode beatific.

Berries in Autumn

Autumn

I am busy, I am bustling,
My gay leafy robes are rustling,
I am scattering my treasures all around;
I bring aliment nutritious,
I bring many fruits delicious,
Where I shake my lap can sumptuous fare be found.

Not within great lordly castles
Do I hang my golden tassels
But in fields where they my landscape scenes enhance;
To tall stem-tops I append them
Where the dew-drops may befriend them
And the playful little sunbeams round them dance.

From high sprays I dangle cherries,
Near the ground I strew bright berries
As I pass through every garden, lane, and grove,
And to tiny twigs I bind them,
Where the little ones can find them
When through my delightful wonderland they rove.

There are many variations
In my orchard decorations,
At new draperies and styles I work apace;
Mellow tints I spread on quickly,
Juicy bulbs I scatter thickly,
And affix each one securely in its place.

I am clever at devising
Something pleasant and surprising,
I hide heaps of good things safely in the soil,
And it's really most intriguing
For my treasures to be digging
'Tis a happy healthy hopeful kind of toil.

All my goods are parcelled neatly,
All are immunized completely,
Special wrappers for each species I provide,
And the many-coloured jackets
Of these dainty little packets
Though unlabelled clearly tell one what's inside.

Then whole landscapes must be painted,
And I must become acquainted
With each tiny nook that all may harmonize,
But I am so energetic,
And my taste is so aesthetic
That my pictures never fail to take the prize.

When my work has been inspected
And my goods have been collected,
I shall sweep the world with wind, my monster broom,
And before I go I'll swash it,
And I'll strip it bare and wash it,
Then bleak Winter may her frosty work resume.

Though I work with zeal so fervent
I am really a servant
I obey the One who sits on Heaven's throne;
I have simply told my story
But to Him is due the glory
For the gifts which I distribute are His own.

Leaving Tirglasson

The house is empty, desolate,
  The furniture is mostly gone;
The night is dark, the hour is late,
  And I am left alone, alone.

No stove, no fire, no friendly face,
  No comfort for my aching heart
Within this solitary place
  From which I too shall soon depart.

My loneliness no words can tell,
  My heart is sick, and sad, and sore;
This was the home I loved so well,
  But now I feel 'tis home no more.

The rooms are dreary, cold, and bare,
  The signs of comfort all are gone;
My footfall loud upon the stair
  Calls forth a sigh, an inward groan.

Outside, the tempest loud proclaims
  Its wrath, and its malignant power,
And loudly on the window panes
  Beats every frequent heavy shower.

I may retire, but not to sleep,
  So agitated is my mind;
I only want to weep and weep
  Because in tears relief I find.

Looking towards Tirglasson

What though another home awaits
   My presence, yet this awful gloom
All future joy obliterates
   For present woes do hopes consume.

But when as in the days of yore
   A happy home I shall possess,
I shall appreciate it more
   For having known such loneliness.

The painful darkness in advance
   Will make that other home more bright,
Thus do the woes of earth enhance
   The glories of the Home of Light.

Part of the old road home from Dungiven to Straid

The Journey Home

Gone was the bus, and Despair dashed down over me;
  Bitter the tears which I wanted to weep.
No roof from chill frosty breezes to cover me!
  Nothing to sit on, and nowhere to sleep!

There in Dungiven all lone and lugubrious,
  Miles between me and the comforts of home,
Far from its atmosphere sweet and salubrious,
  During the dark hours, oh! where could I roam?

Visions I had which were gloomy and horrible –
  Visions of walking the streets all the night,
But to attempt to go home was more terrible,
  Darkness was there – in the streets there was light.

Few were the lamps, and amid so much eeriness
  Pacing the pavements seemed most indiscreet,
Also I feared that with strain and with weariness,
  I should grow faint, and collapse on the street.

Then I bethought me of one I'd met previously,
  One whom I knew might be found in the church;
'Twere a relief to tell some one how grievously
  I had been foiled, and was left in the lurch.

He knew the people, and he might procure for me
  Room on a cart, or a lorry or car,
Any contraption which would but assure for me
  Safety although it might not take me far.

I would have paid any driver unsparingly
   Had I been part of the distance conveyed,
Then would have trudged the remaining miles daringly,
   Lured by the thought of arriving at Straid.

Found was that friend, and of pending calamity
   He was informed, but he smiled at my plight,
Then he assured me with wonderful amity
   That his own car would make matters all right.

What a relief! It seemed almost a miracle
   That a swift car should convey me to Straid!
I who with grief had been almost hysterical
   Thanked and blessed him who my fears had allayed.

Then to increase my surprise and beatitude,
   His winsome lady accompanied us.
How my heart swelled with delight and with gratitude!
   O what a joy to be driven home thus!

Homeward we went with the greatest rapidity,
   Pleasantly chatting and sitting at ease;
After my blunders and all my stupidity
   Why did God send me such good friends as these?

Soon we arrived at this place of felicity,
   Where I can sweetly relax and repose,
Where in delightful secluded simplicity,
   Far from town-turmoil life pleasantly flows.

Gratefully sang I a heart-felt doxology;
   Fervently prayed I that these friends might reap
Manifold blessings. In quaint phraseology
   Praise and prayer mingled till I fell asleep.

But that slight incident fraught with such fearfulness
Has been a boon and a balm to my soul;
It has shed over me sunshine and cheerfulness,
Chasing the clouds which so darkly did roll.

For I had dreaded long months of debility,
On the last lap of my pilgrimage here;
I who had journeyed with so much agility,
Shrank from a check in my active career.

Now though Old Age sometimes pinches me painfully,
Her doleful forecasts my peace do not mar;
I treat her dismal suggestions disdainfully
For I'm expecting a plane or a car.

Fancy still sees the future, but not apprehensively,
For since my Lord sent a car on that night,
He may send one to bring me inexpensively
And swiftly from earth to the city of light.

But there's a manner of going more glorious;
Travelling by car could not with it compare;
Christ may return as a King all-victorious;
I may be caught up to Him in the air.

Now the last lap with this bright hope is glistening
For it may be with this great event crowned;
'Tis for His call I am longing and listening;
Maybe to-day the glad trumpet will sound.

Words of encouragement has my Lord spoken to me,
Words which have brought exultation and rest.
Was not that car His own mystical token to me
Of a swift flight to the realms of the blest?